Anonymous

Saint Paul

Anonymous

Saint Paul

ISBN/EAN: 9783337335908

Printed in Europe, USA, Canada, Australia, Japan

Cover: Foto ©Lupo / pixelio.de

More available books at **www.hansebooks.com**

SAINT PAUL.

.

"There is neither Jew nor Greek, there is neither bond nor free, there is neither male nor female: for ye are all one in Christ Jesus."

CHRIST! I am Christ's ! and let the name suffice you,

Ay, for me too He greatly hath sufficed:

Lo with no winning words I would entice you,

Paul has no honour and no friend but Christ.

Yes, without cheer of sister or of daughter,

Yes, without stay of father or of son,

Lone on the land and homeless on the water

Pass I in patience till the work be done.

Yet not in solitude if Christ anear me
  Waketh him workers for the great employ,
Oh not in solitude, if souls that hear me
  Catch from my joyaunce the surprise of joy.

Hearts I have won of sister or of brother
  Quick on the earth or hidden in the sod,
Lo every heart awaiteth me, another
  Friend in the blameless family of God.

What was their sweet desire and subtle yearning,
  Lovers, and ladies whom their song enrols?
Faint to the flame which in my breast is burning,
  Less than the love with which I ache for souls.

.

Yet it was well, and Thou hast said in season
  'As is the master shall the servant be':
Let me not subtly slide into the treason,
  Seeking an honour which they gave not Thee;

Never at even, pillowed on a pleasure,
  Sleep with the wings of aspiration furled,
Hide the last mite of the forbidden treasure,
  Keep for my joys a world within the world;—

Nay but much rather let me late returning
  Bruised of my brethren, wounded from within,
Stoop with sad countenance and blushes burning,
  Bitter with weariness and sick with sin,—

Then as I weary me and long and languish,
　Nowise availing from that pain to part,—
Desperate tides of the whole great world's anguish
　Forced thro' the channels of a single heart,—

Straight to thy presence get me and reveal it,
　Nothing ashamed of tears upon thy feet,
Show the sore wound and beg thine hand to heal it,
　Pour thee the bitter, pray thee for the sweet.

Then with a ripple and a radiance thro' me
　Rise and be manifest, o Morning Star!
Flow on my soul, thou Spirit, and renew me,
　Fill with Thyself, and let the rest be far.

Safe to the hidden house of thine abiding
　Carry the weak knees and the heart that faints,
Shield from the scorn and cover from the chiding,
　Give the world joy, but patience to the saints.

Saint, did I say? with your remembered faces,

    Dear men and women, whom I sought and slew !

Ah when we mingle in the heavenly places

    How will I weep to Stephen and to you !

Oh for the strain that rang to our reviling

    Still, when the bruised limbs sank upon the sod,

Oh for the eyes that looked their last in smiling,

    Last on this world here, but their first on God !

Let no man think that sudden in a minute

   All is accomplished and the work is done;—

Though with thine earliest dawn thou shouldst begin it

   Scarce were it ended in thy setting sun.

Oh the regret, the struggle and the failing!

   Oh the days desolate and useless years!

Vows in the night, so fierce and unavailing!

   Stings of my shame and passion of my tears!

How have I seen in Araby Orion,
    Seen without seeing, till he set again,
Known the night-noise and thunder of the lion,
    Silence and sounds of the prodigious plain !

How have I knelt with arms of my aspiring
    Lifted all night in irresponsive air,
Dazed and amazed with overmuch desiring,
    Blank with the utter agony of prayer !

Shame on the flame so dying to an ember !
    Shame on the reed so lightly overset !
Yes, I have seen him, can I not remember ?
    Yes, I have known him, and shall Paul forget ?

I, even I who from the fleshly prison
    Caught, (I believe it but I dare not say,)
Rose to the mid light of the Lord arisen,
    Woke to the waking rapture of the day,—

Ah they are shut, the ears of my divining,

  Sealed are the eyes that should have seen Him then:

Look what a beam from the Beloved shining!

  Look what a night of treasonable men!

What was their tale of some one on a summit,

  Looking, I think, upon the endless sea,—

One with a fate, and sworn to overcome it,

  One who was fettered and who should be free?

Round him a robe, for shaming and for searing,

  Ate with empoisonment and stung with fire,

He thro' it all was to his lord uprearing

  Desperate patience of a brave desire.

Ay and for me there shot from the beginning

  Pulses of passion broken with my breath;

Oh thou poor soul, enwrapped in such a sinning,

  Bound in the shameful body of thy death!

Well, let me sin, but not with my consenting,

Well, let me die, but willing to be whole:

Never, o Christ,—so stay me from relenting,—

Shall there be truce betwixt my flesh and soul.

Oft shall that flesh imperil and outweary
  Soul that would stay it in the straiter scope,
Oft shall the chill day and the even dreary
  Force on my heart the frenzy of a hope :—

Lo as some ship, outworn and overladen,
  Strains for the harbour where her sails are furled ;—
Lo as some innocent and eager maiden
  Leans o'er the wistful limit of the world,

Dreams of the glow and glory of the distance,
  Wonderful wooing and the grace of tears,
Dreams with what eyes and what a sweet insistance
  Lovers are waiting in the hidden years ;—

Lo as some venturer, from his stars receiving

    Promise and presage of sublime emprise,

Wears evermore the seal of his believing

    Deep in the dark of solitary eyes,

Yea to the end, in palace or in prison,

    Fashions his fancies of the realm to be,

Fallen from the height or from the deeps arisen,

    Ringed with the rocks and sundered of the sea ;—

So even I, and with a heart more burning,

    So even I, and with a hope more sweet,

Groan for the hour, o Christ! of thy returning,

    Faint for the flaming of thine advent feet.

Ah what a hope! and when afar it glistens
   Stops the heart beating and the lips are dumb;
Inly my spirit to His silence listens,
   Faints till she find Him, quivers till He come.

Once for a night and day upon the splendid
   Anger and solitude of seething sea
Almost I deemed mine agony was ended,
   Nearly beheld Thy Paradise and Thee,—

Saw the deep heaving into ridges narrow,
   Heard the blast bellow on its ocean-way,
Felt the soul freed and like a flaming arrow
   Sped on Euroclydon thro' death to day.

Ah but not yet he took me from my prison,—

Left me a little while, nor left for long,—

Bade as one buried, bade as one arisen

Suffer with men and like a man be strong.

What can we do, o'er whom the unbeholden
 Hangs in a night with which we cannot cope?
What but look sunward, and with faces golden
 Speak to each other softly of a hope?

Can it be true, the grace He is declaring?
 Oh let us trust Him, for his words are fair!
Man, what is this, and why art thou despairing?
 God shall forgive thee all but thy despair.

Truly He cannot, after such assurance,
 Truly He cannot and He shall not fail;
Nay, they are known, the hours of thine endurance,
 Daily thy tears are added to the tale:

Never a sigh of passion or of pity,
Never a wail for weakness or for wrong,
Has not its archive in the angels' city,
Finds not its echo in the endless song.

Not as one blind and deaf to our beseeching,
Neither forgetful that we are but dust,
Not as from heavens too high for our up-reaching,
Coldly sublime, intolerably just :—

Nay but thou knewest us, Lord Christ thou knowest,
Well thou rememberest our feeble frame,
Thou canst conceive our highest and our lowest,
Pulses of nobleness and aches of shame.

Therefore have pity !—not that we accuse thee,
Curse thee and die and charge thee with our woe :
Not thro' thy fault, o Holy One, we lose thee,
Nay, but our own,—yet hast thou made us so !

Then tho' our foul and limitless transgression

  Grows with our growing, with our breath began,

Raise thou the arms of endless intercession,

  . Jesus, divinest when thou most art man !

Also I ask, but ever from the praying

　　Shrinks my soul backward, eager and afraid,

Point me the sum and shame of my betraying,

　　Show me, o Love, thy wounds which I have made!

Yes, thou forgivest, but with all forgiving

　　Canst not renew mine innocence again:

Make thou, o Christ, a dying of my living,

　　Purge from the sin but never from the pain!

So shall all speech of now and of to-morrow,

　　All he hath shown me or shall show me yet,

Spring from an infinite and tender sorrow,

　　Burst from a burning passion of regret:

Standing afar I summon you anigh him,

   Yes, to the multitudes I call and say,

'This is my King! I preach and I deny him,

   Christ! whom I crucify anew to-day.'

Thou with strong prayer and very much entreating
 Willest be asked, and thou shalt answer then,
Show the hid heart beneath creation beating,
 Smile with kind eyes and be a man with men.

Were it not thus, o King of my salvation,
 Many would curse to thee and I for one,
Fling thee thy bliss and snatch at thy damnation,
 Scorn and abhor the shining of the sun,

Ring with a reckless shivering of laughter
 Wroth at the woe which thou hast seen so long,
Question if any recompense hereafter
 Waits to atone the intolerable wrong:

Is there not wrong too bitter for atoning?
　　What are these desperate and hideous years?
Hast Thou not heard Thy whole creation groaning,
　　Sighs of the bondsmen, and a woman's tears?

Yes, and to her, the beautiful and lowly,
　　Mary a maiden, separate from men,
Camest thou nigh and didst possess her wholly,
　　Close to thy saints, but thou wast closer then.

Once and for ever didst thou show thy chosen,
　　Once and for ever magnify thy choice;—
Scorched in love's fire or with his freezing frozen,
　　Lift up your hearts, ye humble, and rejoice!

Not to the rich He came and to the ruling,
　　(Men full of meat, whom wholly He abhors,)
Not to the fools grown insolent in fooling
　　Most, when the lost are dying at the doors;

Nay but to her who with a sweet thanksgiving
  Took in tranquillity what God might bring,
Blessed Him and waited, and within her living
  Felt the arousal of a Holy Thing.

Ay for her infinite and endless honour
  Found the Almighty in this flesh a tomb,
Pouring with power the Holy Ghost upon her,
  Nothing disdainful of the Virgin's womb.

East the forefront of habitations holy
　　Gleamed to Engedi, shone to Eneglaim :
Softly thereout and from thereunder slowly
　　Wandered the waters, and delayed, and came.

Then the great stream, which having seen he showeth,
　　Hid from the wise but manifest to him,
Flowed and arose, as when Euphrates floweth,
　　Rose from the ankles till a man might swim.

Even with so soft a surge and an increasing,
　　Drunk of the sand and thwarted of the clod,
Stilled and astir and checked and never-ceasing
　　Spreadeth the great wave of the grace of God;

Bears to the marishes and bitter places
  Healing for hurt and for their poisons balm,
Isle after isle in infinite embraces
  Floods and enfolds and fringes with the palm.

Ay and afar to realms and to recesses
  Seen in a storm, discovered in a dream,
Fields which no folk nor any power possesses,
  Oceans ungirdled of the ocean-stream :—

Yes or if loose and free, as some are telling,
  (Little I know it and I little care,)
This my poor lodge, my transitory dwelling,
  Swings in the bright deep of the endless air,—

Round it and round His prophets shall proclaim Him,
  Springing thenceforth and hurrying therethro',—
Each to the next the generations name Him,
  Honour unendingly and know anew.

Great were his fate who on the earth should linger,
 Sleep for an age and stir himself again,
Watching Thy terrible and fiery finger
 Shrivel the falsehood from the souls of men.

Oh that thy steps among the stars would quicken!
 Oh that thine ears would hear when we are dumb!
Many the hearts from which the hope shall sicken,
 Many shall faint before thy kingdom come.

Lo for the dawn, (and wherefore wouldst thou screen it?)
 Lo with what eyes, how eager and alone,
Seers for the sight have spent themselves, nor seen it,
 Kings for the knowledge, and they have not known.

Times of that ignorance with eyes that slumbered

Seeing He saw not, till the days that are,

Now, many multitudes whom none hath numbered,

Seek Him and find Him, for He is not far.

Ay and ere now, a triumph and a token,

Flown o'er the severance of the sundering deep,

Came there who called, and with the message spoken

Followed the winging of the ways of sleep.

Ay and ere now above the shining city

Full of all knowledge and a God unknown

Stood I and spake, and passion of my pity

Drew Him from heaven and showed Him to His own.

Heard ye of her who faint beneath the burthen
  Strained to the cross and in its shadow fell?
Love for a love, the angels' for the earthen,—
  Ah, what a secret for the heavens to tell!

She as one wild, whom very stripes enharden,
  Leapt many times from torture of a dream,
Shrank by the loathly olives of the garden,
  Groves of a teacher, and Ilissus' stream:

Then to their temple Damaris would clamber,
  Stood where an idol in the lifted sky
Bright in a light and eminent in amber
  Heard not, nor pitied her, nor made reply.

Thence the strong soul, which never power can pinion,
  Sprang with a wail into the empty air;
Thence the wide eyes upon a hushed dominion
  Looked in a fierce astonishment of prayer:

Looked to Hymettus.and the purple heather,

    Looked to Peiræus and the purple sea,

Blending of waters and of winds together,

    Winds that were wild and waters that were free.

So from the soft air, infinite and pearly,

    Breathed a desire with which she could not cope,

Could not, methinks, so eager and so early,

    Chant to her loveliness the dirge of hope ;

Could not have done with weeping and with laughter

    Leaving men angry and sweet love unknown ;

Could not go forth upon a blank hereafter

    Weak and a woman, aimless and alone.

Therefore with set face and with smiling bitter

    Took she the anguish, carried it apart ;—

Ah, to what friend to speak it ? it were fitter

    Thrust in the aching hollows of her heart.

Then I preached Christ: and when she heard the
　　story,—
Oh, is such triumph possible to men?
Hardly, my King, had I beheld Thy glory,
　　Hardly had known Thine excellence till then.

Thou in one fold the afraid and the forsaken,—
　　Thou with one shepherding canst soothe and save;
Speak but the word! the Evangel shall awaken
　　Life in the lost, the hero in the slave.

Surely one star above all souls shall brighten
  Leading for ever where the Lord is laid ;
One revelation thro' all years enlighten
  Steps of bewilderment and eyes afraid.

Us with no other gospel thou ensnarest,
  Fiend from beneath or angel from above!
Knowing one thing the sacredest and fairest,—
  Knowing there is not anything but Love.

Ay, and when Prophecy her tale hath finished,
  Knowledge hath withered from the trembling tongue,
Love shall survive and Love be undiminished,
  Love be imperishable, Love be young.

Love that bent low beneath his brother's burden,

 How shall he soar and find all sorrows flown!

Love that ne'er asked for answer or for guerdon,

 How shall he meet eyes sweeter than his own!

Love was believing,—and the best is truest;

 Love would hope ever,—and the trust was gain;

Love that endured shall learn that thou renewest

 Love, even thine, o Master! with thy pain.

Not in soft speech is told the earthly story,

 Love of all Loves! that showed thee for an hour;

Shame was thy kingdom, and reproach thy glory,

 Death thine eternity, the Cross thy power.

Oh to have watched thee thro' the vineyards wander,

Pluck the ripe ears, and into evening roam!—

Followed, and known that in the twilight yonder

Legions of angels shone about thy home!

Thunder the message that to me thou gavest;

Writ with the lightning in the skies it ran;

Shepherd of souls! it is not thus thou savest;

Nay, but with sorrows of the Son of Man.

Ah with what bitter triumph had I seen them,

Drops of redemption bleeding from thy brow!

Thieves, and a culprit crucified between them,

All men forsaking him,—and that was Thou!

Oft when the Word is on me to deliver

Opens the heaven and the Lord is there;

Desert or throng, the city or the river,

Melt in a lucid Paradise of air,—

Only like souls I see the folk thereunder,

Bound who should conquer, slaves who should

be kings,—

Hearing their one hope with an empty wonder,

Sadly contented in a show of things;—

Then with a rush the intolerable craving

Shivers throughout me like a trumpet-call,—

Oh to save these! to perish for their saving,

Die for their life, be offered for them all!

Once for the least of children of Manasses
   God had a message and a deed to do,
Wherefore the welcome that all speech surpasses
   Called him and hailed him greater than he knew;

Asked him no more, but followed him and found him,
   Filled him with valour, slung him with a sword,
Bade him go on until the tribes around him
   Mingled his name with naming of the Lord.

Also of John a calling and a crying
   Rang in Bethabara by Jordan's flow;
Art thou the Christ? they asked of his denying;
   Art thou that Prophet? and he answered, No.

John, than which man a sadder or a greater
　Not till this day has been of woman born,
John like some lonely peak by the Creator
　Fired with the red glow of the rushing morn.

This when the sun shall rise and overcome it
　Stands in his shining desolate and bare,
Yet not the less the inexorable summit
　Flamed him his signal to the happier air.

This is His will: He takes and He refuses,
　Finds him ambassadors whom men deny,
Wise ones nor mighty for his saints He chooses,
　No, such as John or Gideon or I.

He as He wills shall solder and shall sunder,
　Slay in a day and quicken in an hour,
Tune him a music from the Sons of Thunder,
　Forge and transform my passion into power.

Ay, for this Paul, a scorn and a reviling,

Weak as you know him and the wretch you see,—

Even in these eyes shall ye behold His smiling,

Strength in infirmities and Christ in me.

Often for me between the shade and splendour
 Ceos and Tenedos at dawn were grey;
Welling of waves, disconsolate and tender,
 Sighed on the shore and waited for the day.

Then till the bridegroom from the east advancing
 Smote him a waterway and flushed the lawn,
God with sweet strength, with terror, and with trancing,
 Spake in the purple mystery of dawn.

Oh what a speech, and greater than our learning!
 Scarcely remembrance can the joy renew:
What were they then, the sights of our discerning,
 Sorrows we suffer, and the deeds we do?

Lo every one of them was sunk and swallowed,

Morsels and motes in the eternal sea,

Far was the call, and farther as I followed

Grew there a silence round the Lord and me.

Oh could I tell ye surely would believe it!
Oh could I only say what I have seen!
How should I tell or how can ye receive it,
How, till He bringeth you where I have been?

Therefore, o Lord, I will not fail nor falter,
Nay but I ask it, nay but I desire,
Lay on my lips thine embers of the altar,
Seal with the sting and furnish with the fire;

Give me a voice, a cry and a complaining,—
Oh let my sound be stormy in their ears!
Throat that would shout but cannot stay for straining,
Eyes that would weep but cannot wait for tears.

Quick in a moment, infinite for ever,

   Send an arousal better than I pray,

Give me a grace upon the faint endeavour,

   Souls for my hire and Pentecost to-day!

Lo as some bard on isles of the Aegean
    Lovely and eager when the earth was young,
Burning to hurl his heart into a paean,
    Praise of the hero from whose loins he sprung ;—

He, I suppose, with such a care to carry,
    Wandered disconsolate and waited long,
Smiting his breast, wherein the notes would tarry,
    Chiding the slumber of the seed of song :

Then in the sudden glory of a minute
    Airy and excellent the proëm came,
Rending his bosom, for a god was in it,
    Waking the seed, for it had burst in flame.

SAINT PAUL

So even I athirst for his inspiring,
   I who have talked with Him forget again;
Yes, many days with sobs and with desiring
   Offer to God a patience and a pain;

Then thro' the mid complaint of my confession,
   Then thro' the pang and passion of my prayer,
Leaps with a start the shock of his possession,
   Thrills me and touches, and the Lord is there.

Lo if some pen should write upon your rafter
   Mene and mene in the folds of flame,
Think ye could any memories thereafter
   Wholly retrace the couplet as it came?

Lo if some strange intelligible thunder
   Sang to the earth the secret of a star,
How should ye catch, for terror and for wonder,
   Shreds of the story that was pealed so far?

Scarcely I catch the words of his revealing,
  Hardly I hear Him, dimly understand,
Only the Power that is within me pealing
  Lives on my lips and beckons to my hand.

Whoso hath felt the Spirit of the Highest
  Cannot confound nor doubt Him nor deny:
Yea with one voice, o world, tho' thou deniest,
  Stand thou on that side, for on this am I.

Rather the earth shall doubt when her retrieving
  Pours in the rain and rushes from the sod,
Rather than he for whom the great conceiving
  Stirs in his soul to quicken into God.

Ay, tho' thou then shouldst strike him from his glory
  Blind and tormented, maddened and alone;
Even on the cross would he maintain his story,
  Yes and in hell would whisper, I have known.

God, who at sundry times in manners many

    Spake to the fathers and is speaking still,

Eager to find if ever or if any

    Souls will obey and hearken to His will;—

Who that one moment has the least descried Him,

    Dimly and faintly, hidden and afar,

Doth not despise all excellence beside Him,

    Pleasures and powers that are not and that are,—

Ay amid all men bear himself thereafter
  Smit with a solemn and a sweet surprise,
Dumb to their scorn and turning on their laughter
  Only the dominance of earnest eyes?—

God, who whatever frenzy of our fretting
  Vexes sad life to spoil and to destroy,
Lendeth an hour for peace and for forgetting,
  Setteth in pain the jewel of his joy:—

Gentle and faithful, tyrannous and tender,
  Ye that have known Him, is He sweet to know?
Softly he touches, for the reed is slender,
  Wisely enkindles, for the flame is low.

God, who when Enoch on the earth was holy
  Saved him from death and Noe from the sea,
Planned Him a purpose that should ripen slowly,
  Found in Chaldæa the elect Chaldee,—

God, who for sowing of the seed thereafter

Called him from Charran, summoned him from Ur,

Gave to his wife a weeping and a laughter,

Light to the nations and a son for her,—

God, who in Israel's bondage and bewailing

Heard them and granted them their heart's desire,

Clave them the deep with power and with prevailing,

Gloomed in the cloud and glowed into the fire,

Fed them with manna, furnished with a fountain,

Followed with waves the raising of the rod,

Drew them and drave, till Moses on the mountain

Died of the kisses of the lips of God;—

God, who was not in earth when it was shaken,

Could not be found in fury of the flame,

Then to his seer, the faithful and forsaken,

Softly was manifest and spake by name,

Showed him a remnant barred from the betrayal,
  Close in his Carmel, where the caves are dim,
So many knees that had not bent to Baal,
  So many mouths that had not kissèd him,—

God, who to glean the vineyard of his choosing
  Sent them evangelists till day was done,
Bore with the churls, their wrath and their refusing,
  Gave at the last the glory of His Son:—

Lo as in Eden when the days were seven
  Pison thro' Havilah that softly ran
Bare on his breast the changes of the heaven,
  Felt on his shores the silence of a man:

Silence, for Adam, when the day departed
  Left him in twilight with his charge to keep
Careless and confident and single-hearted
  Trusted in God and turned himself to sleep:

Then in the midnight stirring in his slumber

    Opened his vision on the heights and saw

New without name or ordinance or number,

    Set for a marvel, silent for an awe,

Stars in the firmament above him beaming,

    Stars in the firmament, alive and free,

Stars, and of stars the innumerable streaming,

    Deep in the deeps, a river in the sea;—

These as he watched thro' march of their arising,

    Many in multitudes and one by one,

Somewhat from God with a superb surprising

    Breathed in his eyes the promise of the sun.

So tho' our Daystar from our sight be taken,

    Gone from his brethren, hidden from his own,

Yet in his setting are we not forsaken,

    Suffer not shadows of the dark alone.

Not in the west is Thine appearance ended,

  Neither from night shall Thy renewal be,

Lo, for the firmament in spaces splendid

  Lighteth her beacon-fires ablaze for Thee;—

Holds them and hides and drowns them and discovers,

  Throngs them together, kindles them afar,

Sheweth, o Love, Thy multitude of lovers,

  Souls that shall know Thee and the saints that are.

Look what a company of constellations!

  Say can the sky so many lights contain?

Hath the great earth these endless generations?

  Are there so many purified thro' pain?

These thro' all glow and eminence of glory

  Cry for a brighter, who delayeth long:

Star unto star the everlasting story

  Pours in a splendour, flashes in a song.

Witness the hour when many saints assembled

    Waited the Spirit, and the Spirit came;

Ay with hearts tremulous and house that trembled,

    Ay with cleft tongues, and the Holy Ghost, and flame.

Witness the men whom with a word He gaineth,

    Bold who were base and voiceful who were dumb :—

Battle, I know, so long as life remaineth,

    Battle for all, but these have overcome.

Witness the women, of His children sweetest,—

    Scarcely earth seeth them but earth shall see,—

Thou in their woe Thine agony completest,

    Christ, and their solitude is nigh to Thee.

What is this psalm from pitiable places

    Glad where the messengers of peace have trod?

Whose are these beautiful and holy faces

    Lit with their loving and aflame with God?

Eager and faint, empassionate and lonely,

    These in their hour shall prophesy again :

This is His will who hath endured, and only

    Sendeth the promise where He sends the pain.

Ay unto these distributeth the Giver

    Sorrow and sanctity, and loves them well,

Grants them a power and passion to deliver

    Hearts from the prison-house and souls from hell.

Thinking hereof I wot not if the portal

    Opeth already to my Lord above :

Lo there is no more mortal and immortal,

    Nought is on earth or in the heavens but love.

Hark what a sound, and too divine for hearing,

    Stirs on the earth and trembles in the air !

Is it the thunder of the Lord's appearing?

    Is it the music of His people's prayer?

Surely He cometh, and a thousand voices

  Call to the saints and to the deaf are dumb;

Surely He cometh, and the earth rejoices

  Glad in His coming who hath sworn, I come.

This hath He done and shall we not adore Him?

  This shall He do and can we still despair?

Come let us quickly fling ourselves before Him,

  Cast at his feet the burthen of our care,

Flash from our eyes the glow of our thanksgiving,

  Glad and regretful, confident and calm,

Then thro' all life and what is after living

  Thrill to the tireless music of a psalm.

Yea thro' life, death, thro' sorrow and thro' sinning

  He shall suffice me, for He hath sufficed:

Christ is the end, for Christ was the beginning,

  Christ the beginning, for the end is Christ.

𝕮𝖆𝖒𝖇𝖗𝖎𝖉𝖌𝖊:

PRINTED BY C. J. CLAY, M.A. AND SONS,
AT THE UNIVERSITY PRESS.

www.ingramcontent.com/pod-product-compliance
Lightning Source LLC
Chambersburg PA
CBHW031808090426
42739CB00008B/1207